The Towns We Leave Hate Us Most

defeye

The Towns We Leave Hate Us Most

Published by flipped eye publishing, 2021
Under the defeye series
All Rights Reserved

ISBN-13: 978-1-905233-75-5

Supported using public funding by
ARTS COUNCIL ENGLAND
LOTTERY FUNDED

The Towns We Leave Hate Us Most

Aislinn Evans

Contents | *The Towns We Leave Hate Us Most*

Untitled

Birds are singing
prehistoric protest songs in Kensington, still leafy.
Her hallways are hot, humid, she ruminates -
takes joy in walking her crackling grounds,
grass dry beyond belief.
The lady of the manor knows only one grief:
the dark smatter on her view,
new, rattling shacks,
packed crowded around the town like dandelions
In a soil-war.
Tomorrow, she will plant daffodils
and flatten them.

Exchange

A god came
pulsing; pillar of light
thrust / envelope.
A god came all night.
When dawn broke, clamouring,
He asked me for a sacrifice.
I gave the god a journal, dripping ink.
In His hands it set
alight. And it's gone.

A god came
thrashing; spitting; snake.
Sunk His teeth into my neck and
burned the veins.
The sun rose, pallid, a god asked
what He could take. I gave
a mirror, smooth and bright.
He shattered it. One bite.

A god came
apple, swollen, wet.
At first I choked, and then
He made me whole.
I asked to know the sacrifice,
and received a single seed.
The god said:
"When my seed is grown
and bearing fruit, I will come
and take what I am owed."

Then day came,
and I was gone.

Face

I am in possession of a face that I do not recognise as mine. It leaks from the eyes. I cannot control it.

The leaking sessions increase in volume and conspicuity as they increase in time. However, they are often short, and quiet, and deeply sorrowful. I don't understand why.

I have tried many things to placate the face for which I am responsible; I have washed it, and smiled with it, and given it things that faces like. I have given it sunshine, and masks, but the sunshine turns it red and the masks just make leaking easier. I have considered calling a plumber, but I'm not aware of any that specialise in this particular element of waterworks.

Sometimes, I shout at the face with which I must live, hoping to discipline it into behaving. I squash its nose and slap its cheeks. It leaks more. It soaks my clothes and leaves me short of breath. It believes I hate it, which I don't, I just feel no attachment to this face to which I am attached.

It has leaked again. This time, it was spontaneous, and public, and I ran to the bathroom before it started making noises. I discipline the face to which I am supposed to belong, in the furthest stall. It doesn't listen, the stall smells, it leaks more.

I am acutely aware of the noise it is making, but I wait it out. Sometimes, the face with which I must stay just needs someone to stay with it, quietly, as it is loud. It lasts ten minutes, maybe fifteen.

I mop the face for which I must care with toilet paper, take a deep breath, and open the door. I see a person, wearing a face that I recognise as mine. My face is leaking.

They wipe my eyes with their hands, I don't fight back; I have no control over the face I would call home.

We exchange glances. I leave.

The Process of Releasing, and Thereby Providing Relief From, Strong or Repressed Emotions.

In my mind, there's a field where I kill you.
One bullet, through the head.
The field was ploughed and turned and left to rot,
nettles making stead amongst the rocks
and bits of broken glass that glitter just for us;
abandoned stardust.
The blood is black.

And you're on your knees.

Maybe you plead with me, offer up
apology wet enough to shock,
and glistening gifts for Charon drop - but more likely,
more often,
I prefer it,
when you don't.

And the moon looks away.

And sometimes I say something
meaningful, or sad, of some poetic revenge.
A thirst that you illicit or you quench
and drench myself in artificial closure, sweetened
saturating soil to completion - but more often
I prefer it
when I don't.

In my mind, the silence never broke.

Perfect Lovers

After Untitled (perfect lovers) by Felix Gonzalez-Torres

There's not a lot to say. Your watch beeps in the night.
The light keeps me awake. That's alright.

We are as two clocks.

        ticktick
        ticktick
        ticktick

We are plastic and metal and gears -
we are breathing and bleeding and fearing the oncoming
        ticktick
        ticktick
        ticktick
        ticktick
        ticktick
        ticktick
        ticktick
        tick tick
        tick   tick
        tick tick
        tick   tick
        tick   tick
        tick tick
        tick   tick
        tick   tick
        tick
        ticktick
        tick   tock
        ticktick
        tick
        tick
        tick   tick

```
tick        tick
ticktick
tick                    tick
tick
tick
tick                              tick
tick
tick
tick
tick
tick
tick

tick


tick



tick
```

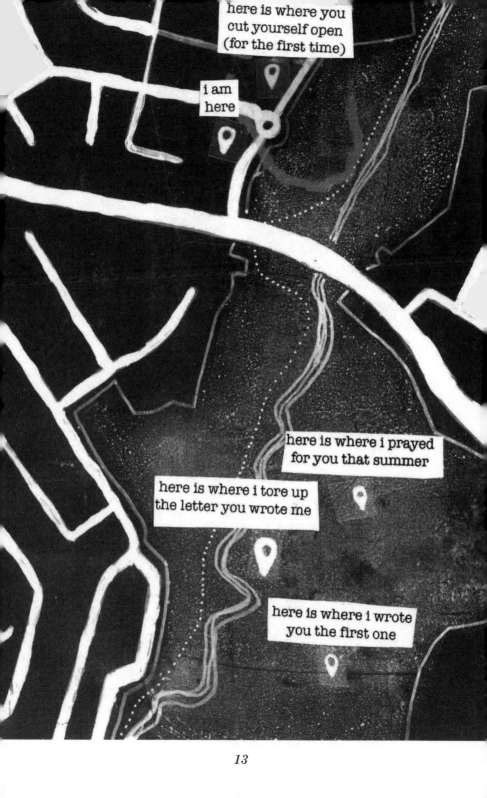

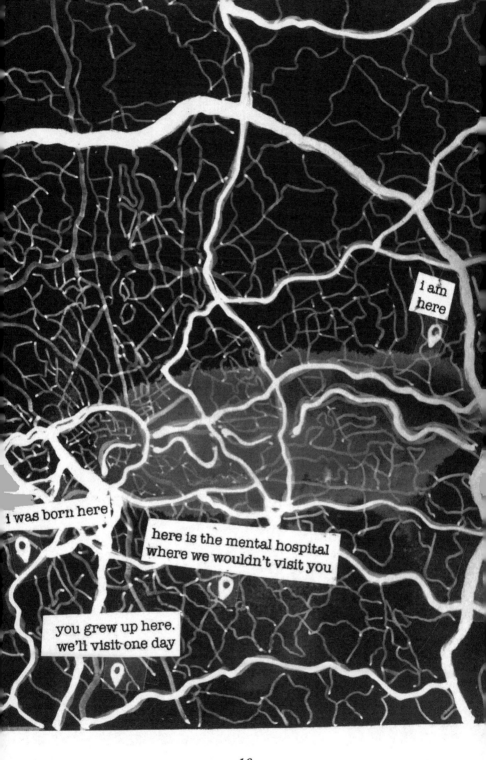

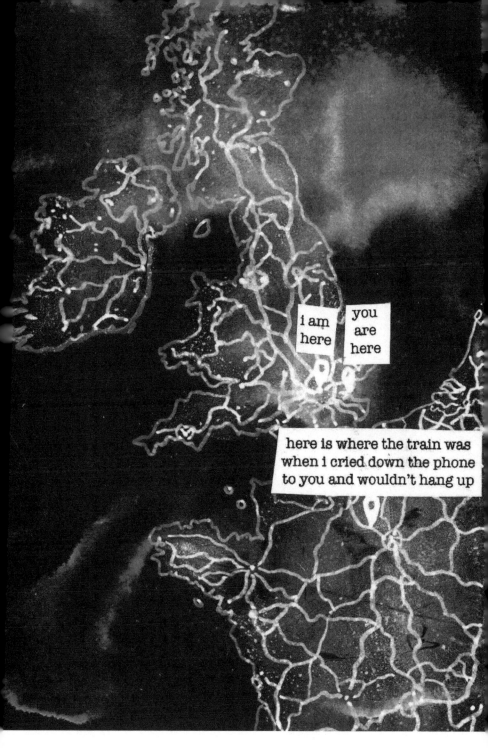

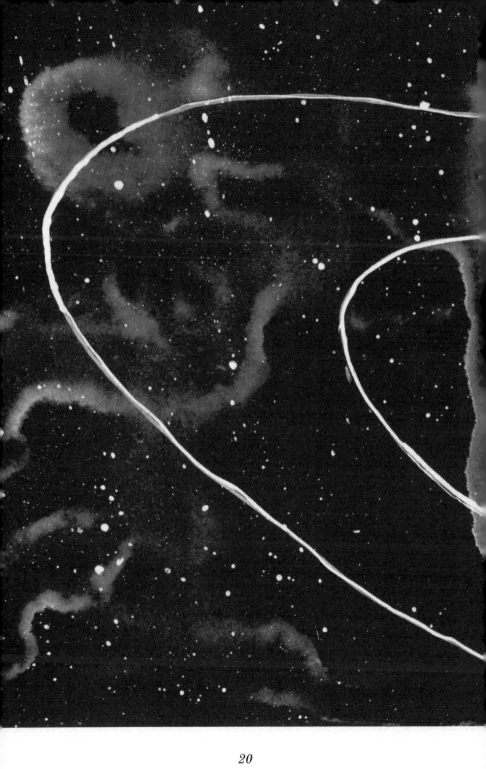

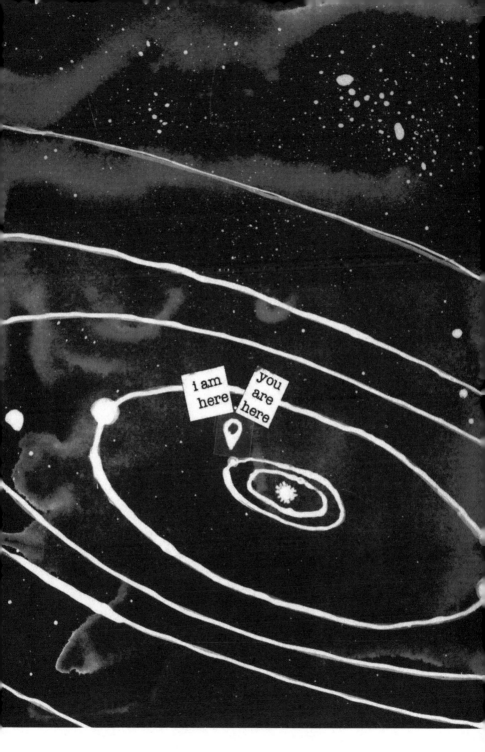

Concrete

a poster liv
these

es between
leaves

The Towns We Leave Hate Us Most

Cut up these cards and shuffle them, read in a circle, or at random.

You walk the subway to the library and hold your breath.

The tower at the centre of town can be seen for miles and does nothing. It's made of asbestos. When it falls, they will evacuate everyone.

You are bored.

Your navigate the maze of interconnected shopping centres. You don't recognise this one. What are you looking for?

Every fence, every lamp post, every tree, is littered with purple ribbons, ragged in the wind. They bleach lilac, bleach violet, bleach baby blue. You forget what it's like without them. You forget her name.

You wonder why nobody recognises you.

You watch a film for £4, the theatre is empty.

Bikes chained up outside the station; one's missing a front wheel, another its seat, the last is just a frame.

You thank God nobody recognises you.

You ride the bus to termination and pull faces at a kid in a pram. Now she won't look away. You did this to yourself.

A child's chatter echoes down the corridor of the shopping centre. This place used to be open air, that's what your dad said.

You are bored.

You walk home with the mother of a girl who made you cry in school. You haven't seen her in years. Keep your distance.

This bus smells like cheap, watery hot chocolate. The kind you share with strangers sheltering from the rain. The kind you had at scout camp, years ago.

You love this town. There is nothing in it to love. You love it because it is there. You love it because it is lonely. You love it because somebody has to.

You ride the train in, look up to watch your old school pass by. You outgrew the rude gestures.

Across from the cemetery. The flats are gravestones. They're coming down soon. Your mum's walls were lined with rats.

You think about endings.

You need to pass by HMV to pick up an NME. It's the last one - ever!

PIGEONS

You think about beginnings.

You share a milkshake with a girl you thought you were desperately in love with. She tries to sell you a phone plan.

The air is thick with chip grease and car exhaust and rain.

You miss the old ice rink.

You go to McDonald's with a girl whose number you will lose.

The trendy new café has been closing for 6 months and counting.

You wonder how long it will be until this place forgets you.

You wait for your bus home.

An illegal quad bike thunders across the bridge

You are hungry.
Hot & Tasty is still open.

Protest Songs

Cut up these cards, stack them in order. In a circle, read them in a round, so that when you have finished card 1, your neighbour reads card 1 while you read card 2. Continue until all the cards have been read out by everyone, perform them however you see fit.

1 WHOSE STREETS?	**2** OUR STREETS.	**3** Justice for Grenfell
4 Alerta Alerta:	**5** Antifascista!	**6** Turn left!
7 Take your masks off.	**8** Who do you serve?	**9** Who do you protect?
10 BORIS JOHNSON	**11** Not my prime minister.	**12** Go back, go back!
13 One solution:	**14** REVOLUTION!	**15** Alerta! Alerta!
16 Antifascista!	**17** Where are you going??	**18** Justice for Grenfell

19 NO BORDERS	**20** NO NATIONS	**21** FUCK DEPORTATION
22 No justice, No peace:	**23** Fuck the police!	**24** Alerta! Alerta!
25 ANTIFASCISTA!	**26** GET BACK!	**27** Get him off the floor.
28 Run!	**29** ALERTA! ALERTA!	**30** We're gonna get kettled!
31 It's too late.		

32

(like a police siren)

WOOOOOOOOOOOOOOOOOOOOOOOOOOOOOO

Generation Loss / Your Language

A game. There is the instigator, and the audience. Sit in any formation that means you can reach each other. The instigator whispers lines one by one into the ear of Audience Member 1, who passes them along one by one. As they reach the final audience member, one by one, she will call out what she hears for the entire audience.

I've learned your language, now watch me fucking curse you in it.

I learned your language, and now look at me as you curse in it.

I learned your language, and now look at me as you are a curse in it.

I learned your language and look at me now because you are cursed.

I learned your language and look at me now because you were cursed.

I learned your language because you are cursed, look at me now.

I study your language because you are cursed to look at me now.

I study your language because you are now curious to look at me.

I am learning your language because you are interested in looking at me now.

I'm learning your language because you're interested in looking at me now.

You are interested in seeing me now, so I am learning your language.